Old Blantyre

by
Rhona Wilson

Suspension Bridge, Bothwell

© Richard Stenlake Publishing 1996
First Published in the United Kingdom, 1996
By Richard Stenlake Publishing, Ochiltree Sawmill, The Lade, Ochiltree, Ayrshire, KA18 2NX. Telephone/fax: 01290 423114

ISBN 1-872074-78-2

GLASGOW ROAD LOOKING EAST, BLANTYRE.

A.6093.

The Sports Centre now stands on the site of the old Blantyre Picture House. Known as 'The Dookit', it was opened in 1913 by Bostock & Sons, a famous (at the time!) circus family. As well as supplying entertainment the owners also seemed to take community involvement seriously, supplying miners with free meals during the general strike of 1926. By 1929 the Picture House was ready to show talkies and was leased out to Leslie Lynn for this purpose the following year. Dorothy Lamour was going down a storm in Jungle Princess towards the end of the decade, around the time this picture was taken. Other cinemas in the area included the Broadway and the 'fleapit' in Forrest Street. Films were also screened at the Co-op Halls from 1916.

INTRODUCTION

The origin of Blantyre's name has caused a few arguments over the centuries. Although the writers of the First and Second Statistical Accounts were agreed that it derived from the Gaelic *Bla'-an-tir* meaning 'a warm retreat', Reverend Mackenzie (writer of the Third Account) derided his predecessors, implying the village was anything but that. He preferred to place emphasis on the local pronunciation 'Blantir' which harks back to the phonetic spelling 'Blantyr' in Blaeu's Map of Scotland, drawn up around 1607. *Tir* or *tyr* in Gaelic means 'land' and he attributes Blan to the name of an early Christian missionary who settled in the area. In conclusion he presents the far more scholarly idea that Blantyre means 'the land of St Blane'.

Whatever the rights or wrongs of the latter theory, the earliest mention of Blantyre can certainly be traced back to religious roots. Blantyre Priory, thought to have been an Augustinian colony of Jedburgh Abbey, was first mentioned in records of the late thirteenth century. During the Reformation the priory was disbanded and gifted to Sir Walter Stewart by King James VI in 1579. He acquired the surrounding lands both by purchase and also as further gifts of the King. Around the beginning of the seventeenth century Blantyre was granted burgh status with the accompanying right to trade its wares - sheep, fish, meal, barley, linen and so on - at weekly and annual markets.

The epitome of a sleepy, rural village, Blantyre surely woke with a start in 1785 when David Dale and James Monteith set up their cotton mills there, catapulting it into the hub of the Industrial Revolution. For centuries Blantyre's stable population of around five hundred had subsisted on agriculture and a little hand-loom weaving, and to a large extent this continued since farm workers were unwilling to put up with factory conditions. The mills, however, needed and got huge numbers of incomers willing to work the long, monotonous hours. By 1801 Blantyre's population had increased by over 200% and continued to rise as the works expanded into Turkey Red Dyeing (a technique for dyeing cotton) and weaving over the first half of the nineteenth century.

By the late 1800s the cotton mill industry was failing, but in 1870 an important discovery was made just in time to save Blantyre. Massive coal deposits were pinpointed where previously there was thought to be only poor quality and difficult to obtain 'sour milk' coal. Six collieries opened providing an income for thousands, including many of the old mill workers. However, this redemption of Blantyre's fortunes was not without cost. In 1877 the worst disaster in the history of Scottish mining occurred when there was an explosion in Dixon's pit, killing over two hundred men. But the population of migrant workers soared regardless, and by 1901 Blantyre's inhabitants numbered a staggering 14,000. Whether the district's development was properly managed is another matter. Newspaper reports of the late nineteenth century described the 'village of a kind' as 'nothing better than a clay hole', with no proper roads or lighting.

However, conditions and communications improved soon enough. Blantyre Gas Works (renonwned for its high prices) opened in Stonefield Road in 1864, and was joined at the beginning of the 1880s by a Water Supply Works. Thirty years later a Refuse Destructor was built, which could consume 45 tons of refuse a day, converting it into electricity in its engine and dynamo room. Blantyre Station was opened in 1849 on the Rutherglen to Hamilton route, with the local wagonettes and omnibuses of the late nineteenth century being taken over by trams in 1903. Housing needs developed in tandem with Blantyre's industries, and mill workers and miners lived in company-built housing near their respective workplaces. Private operators also built two-storey tenements during periods of rapid growth to take advantage of the chronic housing shortage. During the inter-war years, many former fermtouns became the site of local authority housing schemes.

By the 1950s the coal supply was almost completely exhausted and this time there was no saviour industry waiting in the wings. Blantyre was plunged into a long period of unemployment; the population seeping away as miners moved out and the main thoroughfare (Glasgow Road) becoming a run-down and depressing sight. The area had to wait until the 1970s and 80s for redevelopment when the decrepit tenements disappeared and Blantyre got its shopping and sports centres. Although not the most aesthetic of additions, they provided much needed facilities and employment for the area. Formerly an industrial town in its own right, Blantyre now has to rely on its proximity to surrounding towns such as Glasgow and Hamilton for job opportunities.

Blantyre Mills were established by David Dale and James Monteith in the 1780s for the spinning of water twist yarn. The mills expanded steadily throughout the first half of the nineteenth century, with the introduction of Turkey Red dyeing in 1804 (the second such factory in Scotland), and a weaving factory in 1813. However, in the latter half of the nineteenth century the cotton mill industry began to fail. Underinvestment, foreign competition, difficulty in obtaining raw materials, and the break-up of the British Empire all contributed to its demise, and Monteith and Co. finally went into liquidation in 1904. This picture of the Madder Mill, used for Turkey Red dyeing, shows the dilapidated state of the premises at Blantyre around the time of the company's liquidation.

Blantyre Mills, 1903. The bell tower on the roof of the building was probably used for summoning workers at the ungodly hour of 6 a.m. Staff were employed to work 77 hours a week with breaks amounting to less than two hours per day, and although this regime sounds gruelling, conditions were generally believed to be better than industry standards of the time. So-called benefits included the fresh air, cleanliness and 'tar burnt to relieve the smell of oil' in the mills. Nevertheless, Dale and Monteith had difficulty persuading local people to work in the mills, and on one occasion apparently recruited around 200 would-be Highland emigres whose ship was stranded at Greenock, persuading them to settle for Blantyre instead of Canada.

41088

Valentine's Series

A workers' village was built around the mills *c.* 1830, and by 1836 its population was approaching 2,000. Facilities for the self-sufficient mill community included a public washing house, bleaching green, graveyard and school. However, with the decline in the textiles industry, the houses making up the village were allowed to fall into disrepair and were condemned in 1913, although it took another twelve years for the local authority to begin demolishing them. Shuttle Row tenements and the surrounding grounds were eventually bought by the founders of the Livingstone Memorial in 1927.

This *c.* 1903 picture shows the edge of the mill village, now the approach to the David Livingstone Memorial. The village gates stood on this road near the bridge, and were closed every night after a 10 p.m. curfew. The round building on the right is marked as the site of the post office in maps of 1899, but has long since been demolished, along with its partner across the road. Of all the buildings in this shot only those that house what is now the village shop remain. Today, both sides of the road are occupied by modern housing schemes.

DR LIVINGSTON'S SCHOOL BLANTYRE VILLAGE

Blantyre Mill School was built in the late 1820s on a site to the north of the village, and also functioned as a chapel when required. Its most famous pupil was the Victorian missionary David Livingstone, born in 1813. Livingstone started work at the age of ten, working fourteen hours a day as a 'piecer', joining broken threads. Ambitious from an early age, he is said to have read as he worked and finished off his day with a four hour study session. Livingstone's strict Christian upbringing had a strong effect on him and at the age of twenty-four he applied to the London Missionary Society, who accepted him for training two years later. The destination of his first expedition, Africa, was apparently chosen because he could depart for there immediately.

DR. LIVINGSTONE'S BIRTHPLACE, BLANTYRE

Shuttle Row, built around 1780, was home to twenty-four families including David Livingstone's. Conditions were basic, and its turret walls were inset with cast iron 'jaw-boxes' where sewage was deposited, which must have made the approach to the houses particularly unpleasant.

THE BIRTH ROOM, DAVID LIVINGSTONE MEMORIAL, BLANTYRE.

A 6533.

Livingstone's entire family once lived in this tiny room, photographed in the 1920s. The old village grounds were purchased in 1927 to create the David Livingstone Memorial, and two years was spent working on the Shuttle Row tenement before the museum opened. Generations of curators must have used a degree of poetic licence as the room's furnishings have changed considerably with time.

10

Livingstone sailed for Algoa Bay, South Africa, in December 1840. His first stop was a mission station at Kruman in what is now Botswana, and it was there that he met Mary Moffat whom he married in 1845. After Mary died in 1862, Livingstone was commissioned by the British Government and the Royal Geographical Society to locate the source of the Nile. The journalist Henry M. Stanley came across the explorer in Ujiji at Lake Tanganyika in 1871. Despite being too weak to continue his expedition safely, Livingstone refused to return home and died two years later in a hut in Chambito's Village, similar to this replica (photographed in the 1950s). His body was disguised as a package (corpses were considered unlucky) and carried on a nine month journey to the coast before being returned to Britain.

High Blantyre looking towards Auchinraith Road, 1903. The first settlement in Blantyre would have been in the far north of the parish, near to the priory on the banks of the Clyde. However, when the priory was disbanded during the Reformation, the High Blantyre villages of Barnhill, Kirkton and Hunthill developed near the parish church. With the establishment of the mills in the late nineteenth century there was a further population shift. The workers' village became home to the many incomers, and this new settlement led to the distinction between 'High' and 'Low' Blantyre. The thatched cottage in this picture has now been demolished, as has the tenement block beside it, the latter being replaced by a space-age toilet.

HIGH BLANTYRE

BRANDON SERIES

The spire of Blantyre Parish Church is visible in the background of this 1904 picture, taken just beyond the Cross. Its first minister, William Chirnside, was also the last Catholic priest at the priory. The way he changed his beliefs like a pair of socks illustrates the religious turmoil of the Reformation, when scruples went out of the window as people desperately scrabbled to join the 'right' side. The minister who wrote the Second Statistical Account used his position to complain that 'the manse is falling apart', quickly making the point that 'Lord Blantyre is patron'! Almost everything in this picture except the brick wall surrounding the church has gone. A centenary memorial to victims of the colliery disaster stands on the left and there is a sheltered housing scheme to the right.

The name Causeystanes was originally given to a group of tenements surrounding Kirkton Park, and the tenement just visible on the left of this 1905 picture, built in 1894, still bears the name. Today, the view up Broompark Road looks very different. The building next to Causeystanes has been demolished and replaced by a small brick extension to a dental surgery, plus an adjoining car park. There is another car park on the right, and beyond that some small shops and a car salesroom. The wall and trees have also gone and modern houses stand on their site. Main Street is as busy today as it seems to have been when this picture was taken.

High Blantyre.

Blantyre Cross looking down Hunthill Road *c.* 1908, with the old railway bridge in the background. The rounded block on the right was once the church hall. Although this picture of Main Street looks peaceful enough, the *Advertiser* was inundated with letters from outraged residents unhappy about the state of Blantyre's roads around this time, with one man complaining about having to walk ankle-deep through mud in Chapel Street. The reason for this probably lies in Blantyre's spurts of population growth which attracted the private companies who built many of these two-storey tenements. They were erected hastily, often resulting in both sub-standard housing and badly co-ordinated facilities.

The Hamilton and Strathaven Railway opened High Blantyre Station in 1863, although it was taken over by the Caledonian Railway the following year. They ran a service for various industries in the area including Quarter Ironworks, Dixon's Pits and the Blantyre Colliery. In 1885 a connection from High Blantyre to East Kilbride was opened for both freight and passengers. The Strathaven passenger service via High Blantyre ended in 1945, and the freight service ceased eight years later. New houses at Craigmuir Road and Gardens now occupy the approximate site of the station, which stood off Main Street past the Cross. This picture dates from *c.* 1910.

High Blantyre, *c.* 1915. A rose garden now stands on the site of the Station Cafe. From about 1910 housing conditions in Blantyre were said to improve, with dramatic reductions in infant mortality rates reported in some areas, thanks to the County Council improving housing and sewerage. But by the 1930s the situation seemed as bad as ever. In 1938 the *Advertiser* covered a story about nine squatters who faced conviction for living in condemned buildings in Greenside Street and Stonefield Road. But as their lawyer said, what else could they do? The imminence of war had put a stop to the housing schemes that were being built across the country.

The Cross, High, Blantyre.

A great shot of Blantyre Cross facing towards Springwells, taken around 1915. Douglas Street, now widened and forming the feeder route to the East Kilbride Expressway, is on the right. The Station Cafe tenement has been demolished, as have the white tenements to the right of it, although Carrigans pub still stands, and some of Blantyre's old milestones can be seen inside it.

The only means of identifying this picture of Main Street is by the large two-storey building whose gable end is visible at the far end. This is still standing as the Stones Hotel, although everything else in the picture has been demolished. The tenement block containing the bank, post office (run by Mrs Darling) and Dan Dove's butchers shop has been replaced by a new range of facilities housed in a modern brick row.

General's Bridge was named after General Peter of Crossbasket House (opposite). This scene has changed little today, except that there is now less vegetation which has opened up the view at the back.

Crossbasket House, High Blantyre.

Crossbasket House, photographed *c*. 1908. By the 1950s the old mansion house was being let out as flats and was later taken over as a private hospital. Today it is the property of an American religious group, and the sign outside reads 'Christian Centre of the Latter Rain Ministries'. The approach to Crossbasket has changed dramatically over the years; the greenhouses have been removed and the gardens raised to be level with the house - there are no slopes in sight now.

Barnhill was a fermtoun situated at the bend between Bardykes and Hunthill Road. All the buildings in this picture (*c.* 1910), except those on the right, have been demolished and replaced by a parking area for the Clyde Valley Community Forest project. The white gable end on the right of the picture was cut away as part of road-widening works.

Taken a few years earlier than the one opposite, this picture, looking down from Bardykes Road, gives a better view of the Barnhill Tavern; still standing and still quaint. Fifty years ago the proprietor was Nelly Moya, eventually succeeded by Peter MacDonald the piper.

BLANTYRE COTTAGE HOSPITAL

The old cottage hospital stands at no. 63 Bardykes Road, just along from Barnhill. Blantyre had a fever hospital from around 1880, but at the turn of the century local doctors began to appeal for additional resources, and in February 1906 a public meeting was held to discuss methods of raising funds amongst Blantyre residents. Local businessmen such as the coalmasters also made donations, but these were not entirely philanthropic since their workers often needed the facilities of a hospital. Opened in 1910, the hospital was the first of its kind in the county to be paid for by public subscription. Despite an article appearing in the *Gazette* in the 1930s about mineral reserves in its grounds, the building is still standing as a private residence! Local health services are now catered for by the district health centre in Victoria Street.

BLANTYRE ORGAN GRINDERS.

This postcard, dating from around 1908, illustrates two of the methods used to raise funds for the Cottage Hospital. Organ grinders collected cash, while postcards featuring them, such as this one, were sold to raise money too. Specially produced postcards were sold to raise money for a good cause on at least one other occasion in Blantyre. In 1913 John Gray, a miner from Shuttle Row, attempted to rescue twelve year old John Morran who had slipped off a wall into the Clyde while playing with friends. Gray had previously rescued someone in similar circumstances, but having almost reached the embankment he developed cramp and dropped Morran. Both of them drowned. In addition to publishing a postcard, an open air concert and even a football match courtesy of Hamilton Accies were considered as fund-raising options for the man dubbed 'The Blantyre Hero'.

Peth Brae, Blantyre.

Pech Brae (the spelling on this card is wrong), led down to Milheugh House, and appears as Pathfoot on maps of 1899. This steep runway was renamed by locals on account of the vast amounts of 'pech' needed to get up it. Taken in the mid-1920s, this picture shows two estate cottages which have long since been demolished. Part of the wall on the left is still standing and it is still possible to make out the cottage boundaries.

Milheugh House, Blantyre

Milheugh House was in the possession of the Millar family from the fourteenth century onwards. There were originally mills on the land which were a profitable source of income for the family. One time resident Andrew Millar (1735-1801) was Professor of Law at Glasgow University for forty years and the first in Scotland to give lectures in English (previously Latin was used). The house itself lay empty from some time after the late 1920s and was totally derelict by 1954, occupied only by squatters. Since then it has been demolished and the estate developed as a Community Forest Project. There is also a caravan park at the foot of Pech Brae named Niaroo.

Hunthill Road has changed so much since this 1904 picture was taken that the exact spot is difficult to locate. Needless to say all the buildings have been demolished. Village areas such as Kirkton and Hunthill used to be made up of limestone walled thatched cottages such as the one just visible on the left, and a similar cottage stood on Hunthill Road up to the 1950s.

Hunthill Road, Blantyre.

The only building in this picture left standing is the one on the curve with the dormer windows, now the Weaver's Gallery. The shrubs on the left were replaced by modern cottage buildings and fencing some time around the 1930s.

Station Road connected Blantyre Mills to the main Glasgow - Hamilton Road, and the first houses built on it developed out from the main thoroughfare. This picture was taken around 1910, looking towards the Livingstone Memorial. The space on the left has been filled in with another house and the whole of the right hand side has been rebuilt with modern dwellings.

In 1849 the Caledonian Railway opened its Rutherglen - Hamilton route which included a stop at Blantyre. Although originally intended as a goods line for Lanarkshire's coal and iron output, passengers soon became an important source of revenue, and Low Blantyre station was rebuilt in the picturesque form seen here around the turn of the century. In 1974 the route was electrified and the appealing brick and timber station buildings removed and replaced with modern British Rail fittings. More recently, the station has been the subject of a revamping project involving landscaping and the installation of works of art. Nowadays, on a site at the far right hand corner of this picture, two silver men clutching a pole between them can be seen heading in a determined fashion for a nearby flower-bed.

In the mid-nineteenth century Blantyre had thirty-seven heritors, each of whom paid feu-duty to Lord Blantyre for their lands. Usually this took the form of cash, but not in the case of the Bardykes Estate, in possession of the Jackson family from 1525. The Jacksons held on to the lands on the rather bizarre condition that they present Lord Blantyre with a red rose whenever he required; easier in the summer than the depths of winter! Landowners were frequently involved in local decision-making, as is testified by the names of the various Blantyre heritors turning up at meetings for town improvement schemes. J. Wardrope of Greenhall House (above), was often the chair at such meetings and also donated the horse trough that is set into the graveyard wall. The mansion was still standing in the 1930s but has since been demolished.

Glasgow Road serves as a good measure of the changes that have taken place in Blantyre over the last century. This stretch at Stonefield was photographed around 1902 before the advent of trams, chain stores, electric lighting or redevelopment. At one point the Glasgow - Hamilton route was a turnpike road complete with charges for entry into burghs along the way. Turnpikes were usually unmaintained dirt tracks taken over and revamped by landowners who charged dearly for the right to travel on them. Virtually a license to print money (particularly on fair days), this privilege was eventually abolished by parliament in the mid-nineteenth century. Modern redevelopment of the road began in 1929 with widening works.

In 1888 the main form of public conveyance in Blantyre was the wagonette and horse, with not even a bus service available until 1894. However, in 1900 the Tramways Bill authorised a tram route from Blantyre to Wishaw as part of the new development through Motherwell and Hamilton. The five pence service started running in 1903, the same year that this picture was taken, with over 30,000 passengers turning up along the route on the opening day. Both sides of this section of Glasgow Road have now been completely redeveloped. The tenements on the left have been replaced by a low-level housing development, also affecting John Street and Forrest Street. On the opposite side of the road there is now an assortment of modern buildings including industrial units, housing and a shopping centre.

34

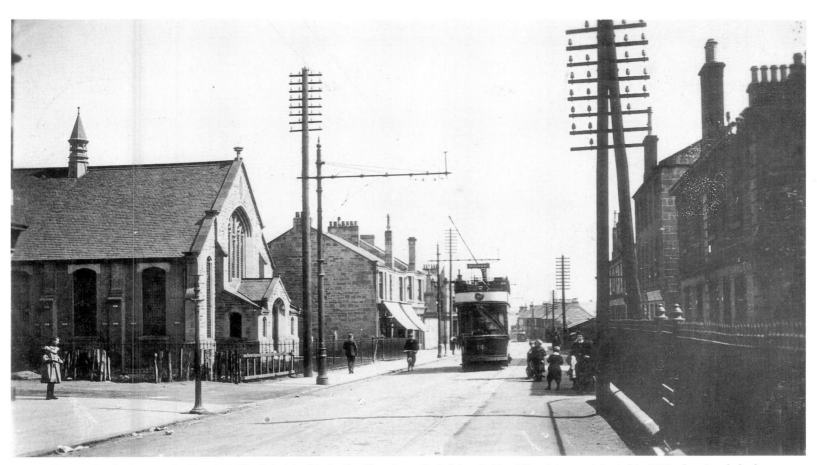

Glasgow Road, photographed in 1908. The Primitive Methodist Church, on the left-hand side of the picture, originated in 1893 when it only had a handful of members. By 1902 services were being held in Dixon's Hall (built by the coal-master of the same name) and the decision to build the Glasgow Road church was taken the following year. The new church opened in 1905 and was in use until the First World War. After lying vacant for a time it was bought by Stonefield Independent Co-op in 1925. It is now called the Bethany Hall and is run by the Christian Brethren, who have been active in Blantyre since the first decade of the century.

Glasgow Road, Blantyre.

(No. 2.)

The large three-storey block on the left of this 1920s picture was Blantyre's Co-op. Communally owned co-operative shops date back to the end of the Napoleonic Wars when they sprung up in industrial areas hit by post-war recession. The main advantage of shopping at a co-op was the annual dividend that they paid out, sometimes equivalent to as much as ten weeks' wages. Blantyre's Co-op was registered in 1883 at a time when the population was expanding rapidly because of the new coal industry. In the early 1940s the wholesome grocers was accused of using child labour but it survived the scandal and was integrated into the SCWS Retail Group in 1972, when it lost the Co-op label. Today a Co-op funeral parlour and butchers are still housed on the ground floor of the building.

A.6094.

GLASGOW ROAD LOOKING WEST, BLANTYRE.

Glasgow Road in 1937 with a hugely increased traffic flow - although no evidence of any traffic lights. The Church Street tenements on the left have been wiped out, with the Clydeview Shopping Centre built on their site in 1980. The right side of the street has also been totally demolished and brick housing stands on it as far as the junction with John Street. Beyond that there is a football pitch, sports centre and park.

This picture and the one opposite show how a stretch of Glasgow Road changed over a thirty year period. In 1903 there was a patch of waste ground adjacent to Stonefield Church (above), but by the 1930s it had been built up with tenements and shops, obscuring the view of the church. Someone also eventually spruced up the brick tenement facades on the left so that they matched their neighbours' appearance. The transport situation also changed radically, with cars gliding down a newly surfaced road, replacing the trams that had previously rumbled along dirt streets.

GLASGOW ROAD, BLANTYRE

Today this section of Glasgow Road looks radically different from both of these pictures. Stonefield Church, opened in 1880, was destroyed by fire in the late 1970s, just a few years after it was reinvented as St Andrew's. All that remains today is a square of grass where it once stood. The 1930s tenements next to it have also gone, and the site is once again empty. There is now a roundabout about a third of the way up the street, just past Logan Street, and both sides of the road have been redeveloped as far as the eye can see. The long sought-after sports centre now stands on the left.

A.6548.   GLASGOW ROAD, BLANTYRE.

Dating from 1953, the old post office building is still standing, although currently up for sale. A map surveyed in 1859 shows the post office of the time on Station Road, just within the confines of the mill village where most of Blantyre's population resided. The current post office is in the Clydeview Shopping Centre. Opened in 1980 as part of Blantyre's redevelopment, the shopping centre is busy and apparently thriving, although not very easy on the eye.

40

GLASGOW ROAD, BLANTYRE.

A.6546.

The Broadway Cinema in Glasgow Road opened in 1939, and for a time there were fears that it would be requisitioned for the war effort. The first film it showed was 'The Dawn Patrol', starring Errol Flynn and Basil Rathbone. Instead of being turned into a bingo hall, The Broadway was demolished and a modern two-storey building for Blantyre's Housing Department built on its site. At one time, the old turnpike road tollhouse stood directly across from the cinema on Station Road. Placed strategically on the corner so that no-one could sneak past it, the tollhouse probably targeted traffic going to and from the mill village and railway station. The tenement block with the crown feature which replaced it was built in 1902.

STONEFIELD ROAD, BLANTYRE.

Stonefield was the subject of a campaign to elevate it to burgh status in 1878, although the plan didn't get much support from ordinary members of the public who seemed to equate the promotion with nothing other than higher taxes. A poll was eventually held which came out against the issue and had local characters such as Tam Tod gloating that the "fors' had made 'an awfu' show o' themselves'. Today, Stonefield Road looks very different from this 1906 picture. The shrubs on the left are now the site of the Commercial Bar, and J. Struthers' shop has been demolished. Straight ahead is St. Joseph's Church which was demolished and replaced by a new building a little further up Glasgow Road in 1938. The stretch of shops on the right has been replaced by new brick housing.

Auchinraith Rd, Blantyre.

I have to admit that I found this picture, dating from around 1908, impossible to locate. The gateway to High Blantyre, Auchinraith Road has been subject to much redevelopment and building over the course of the twentieth century. The two tenement blocks on the left seem to have been demolished as they are nowhere in evidence. It is quite possible that the houses just beyond them are still standing, but these are difficult to pinpoint because of Blantyre's penchant for pokey-out dormer windows, of which there are countless examples!

The Gardens, Auchentibber. High Blantyre.

The tiny hamlet of Auchentibber, a couple of miles south of High Blantyre, was once a thriving community of around sixty dwellings whose inhabitants worked in the nearby stone quarries. Its wonderful and wacky Italian Gardens were built in a mutually beneficial partnership between J. B. Struthers, the Auchentibber Inn landlord, and local workers. Struthers supplied the cash and the work was done by local miners in conjunction with his nephew Jimmy Green, everyone finishing off with a lucrative pint in the Inn at the end of the night. Amenities were still amazingly sparse as late as the 1950s, residents having to resort to paraffin oil lamps and dry toilets, and this, along with the demise of the quarries, undoubtedly led to Auchentibber's demise. By the time of Struthers' death in 1938 the Gardens were just a memory.

QUOITING GROUND, AUCHINTIBBER, HIGH BLANTYRE

Auchentibber's Quoiting Club was almost as famous as its surrounding gardens, and the village won the Scottish Cup in 1928, twenty years after this picture was taken. Today Auchentibber has shrunk to a handful of houses contained in one tiny street. It still has a substantial war memorial (with pillars from Hamilton Palace), and this marks the start of where the garden walkways would have been. Beyond these, it is possible to make out the flat surface of the former Quoiting Green, now completely overgrown. The other side of the main road was once lined with cottages, although every trace of rubble has now gone and most of the land has reverted to the countryside it started off as. Local complaints centre on the lorries that hurtle past the village at breakneck speed en route to a landfill site, filling the otherwise quiet roads with dust.

45

Spittal Bridge, Blantyre.

Spittal Bridge was probably another name for Priory Bridge, which crosses the Rotten Calder on the A724. The road has been widened since this picture was taken and it is possible that the old bridge has been engulfed by the concrete structure that exists now.

The Priory, Blantyre

The Priory, dating from the thirteenth century or earlier, was situated on the banks of the Clyde opposite Bothwell Castle. One Victorian commentator said of the scene: '. . . what with the stags that bounded through the woods and the salmon that swarmed in the rivers, the jolly priests and peaceful villagers of that old Blantyre must have felt that verily their lives had fallen in pleasant places!' Records state that Friar Walter of Blantyre Priory was involved in negotiating a ransom for King David Bruce when he was a prisoner of the Battle of Durham in 1346, and William Wallace is said to have performed a swashbuckling leap into the Clyde from its walls when interrupted on a visit by some hostile English. The ruins of the Priory can still be visited, although judging by this 1908 picture it seems unlikely that there is much left to see.

47

Blantyre Victoria were reconstructed as a junior team in 1902, playing in the Scottish Central League. The Vics were successful in winning the League Championship in 1935/36 and also contested the final of the Lanarkshire Cup in the same season. Team members, from left to right, back to front are: W. Reid, D. Fletcher, J. Gillespie, J. Lyle, A. Little, A. Williamson. Front row: J. McDougall, T. McGee, R. Moffat, W. Towers (Capt.), C. McNee.

Miner's wife, 1907. The worst mining disaster in Scottish history took place in Blantyre in October 1877 when Dixon's Pit exploded killing over two hundred men. It is thought that the tragedy occurred when a build-up of fire-damp (the equivalent to North Sea gas) was ignited by a naked flame on a miner's hat. High Blantyre was thrown into turmoil as thousands of ghoulish spectators joined the relatives crowding around the pit head as bodies were brought up over the following days. The newspapers too, in the absence of photographs, took to relaying graphic descriptions of the victims' injuries. A public inquiry was organised, but although it was discovered that safety regulations had been flouted no recommendations were made about taking action against the employers. In fact, it laid part of the blame on the miners (unable to defend themselves for obvious reasons) saying that they were responsible for reporting the pit if they considered risks were being taken! It also felt great sympathy for the Dixons stating that 'the owners [were] severe sufferers by the wreck of property and the expense of and delay in restoration'. It seems unlikely that any lessons were learnt. Just two years later there was another explosion killing twenty-eight men.

Broompark Road, High Blantyre.

These smart houses date from the late 1920s/early 1930s and were probably built as part of the 'Homes for Heroes' scheme of the inter-war years. The grubby tenement block at the back has been demolished and is now the garden of a large house.

CHILDREN'S PLAYGROUND, LIVINGSTONE MEMORIAL, BLANTYRE.   221199. J.V.

Livingstone's Park, 1933. Over the decades, the David Livingstone Memorial has become a standard venue for children's outings, although locals comment that no one from Blantyre ever visits it!

Calder Glen, Blantyre.

119/32

Calderglen was one of the Blantyre mansion houses which managed to survive after its heritor residents (including John Richard Cochrane in the late 1880s) deserted it. By the 1950s it was owned by a greyhound racing company, later being taken over as the Calderglen Nursing Home. Today it is structurally intact but looks a little dilapidated - the since-departed ivy seems to have caused some damage.